AMERICA*S ALL-TIME FAVORITE PIANO PIECES

166 BEST-LOVED PIANO SOLOS
COMPILED AND EDITED BY AMY APPLEBY

T0087672

Amsco Publications
A Part of **The Music Sales Group**
New York/London/Paris/Sydney/Copenhagen/Berlin/Tokyo/Madrid

To Dorothy Duncan, for making this book possible

Cover photograph: © Jupiterimages Corporation
Project editor: Felipe Orozco

This book Copyright © 2006, 2008 by Amsco Publications,
A Division of Music Sales Corporation, New York

Order No. AM 994983
International Standard Book Number: 978-0-8256-3666-0

Exclusive Distributors:
Music Sales Corporation
257 Park Avenue South, New York, NY 10010 USA
Music Sales Limited
14-15 Berners Street, London W1T 3LJ England
Music Sales Pty. Limited
20 Resolution Drive, Caringbah, NSW 2229, Australia

Printed in the United States of America by
Vicks Lithograph and Printing Corporation

PREFACE

The piano has long enjoyed a place of honor in the American home. In fact, there was a time when no household was considered to be truly complete without a keyboard instrument in the parlor. Many a happy evening hour was spent gathered around the piano, singing and playing at this "entertainment center" of yesteryear. But unlike the television, the piano has the power to inspire us to a deeper level of creative involvement. For example, most pianists would agree that they have more fun in a few minutes at the piano than watching even the liveliest sitcom.

This comprehensive collection celebrates the ongoing American love affair with piano music, now spanning three centuries. Here you will find the most beautiful and familiar classical masterpieces of Europe, along with America's all-time favorite folk, blues, ragtime, jazz, and Broadway showstoppers. The great keyboard solos of Bach, Beethoven, Mozart, Brahms, Debussy, and Schumann—and the brilliant orchestral works of Haydn, Handel, Tchaikovsky, Saint-Saëns, and Rimsky-Korsakov—are all well-represented in this volume.

The music provided in this collection also celebrates America and her many landscapes—from the Smoky Mountains to the Red River Valley—from the banks of the Wabash to the Swanee River shore. Music played an important role in the early development of all of these regions. In fact, no sooner was a frontier settled by pioneers, than it seemed to also be almost magically furnished with pianos. This proliferation of the instrument in unlikely rural American homesteads caused Emerson to marvel:

> *'Tis wonderful how soon a piano gets into a log hut on the frontier.*
> *You would think they found it under a pine stump.*

The piano was also a mainstay in America's sprawling city landscape, because it provided the backbone of entertainment in saloons, cabarets, and theatres across the country. This collection also traces the rich urban heritage of blues, jazz, and showtunes—from "Way Down Yonder in New Orleans" to "Chicago" and "The Sidewalks of New York."

The piano solos gathered here in this volume have stood the test of time—and most are as popular today as they were a hundred years ago. The arrangements are easy to play—and especially rewarding for the developing pianist. Whenever you sit down to play the great classics in this volume, old or new, you are celebrating a truly great American tradition.

CONTENTS

CLASSICAL GEMS

ROMANTIC FAVORITES

CELEBRATE AMERICA

ALL OVER THIS LAND

JAZZ STANDARDS AND SHOWSTOPPERS

ORCHESTRAL THEMES

Novelty Solos

Hymns and Celebrations

CLASSICAL GEMS

Prelude No. 1

from *The Well-Tempered Clavichord*

Johann Sebastian Bach

Moderato

Prelude No. 2

from *Twelve Little Preludes*

Johann Sebastian Bach

Allegro non troppo

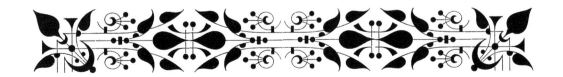

March

from *The Little Notebook of Anna Magdalena Bach*

Johann Sebastian Bach

Allegro maestoso

Minuet

from *The Little Notebook of Anna Magdalena Bach*

Johann Sebastian Bach

Moderato

Musette

from *The Little Notebook of Anna Magdalena Bach*

Johann Sebastian Bach

Moderato

Two-Part Invention No. 1

Johann Sebastian Bach

Allegro

Two-Part Invention No. 8

Johann Sebastian Bach

Vivace

Für Elise

Ludwig van Beethoven

Poco moto

(Ped. simile)

Minuet in G

Ludwig van Beethoven

Moderato

Moonlight Sonata

Ludwig van Beethoven

Adagio sostenuto

Sonata in G

Ludwig van Beethoven

Allegro, ma non troppo

Sonata Pathétique

Ludwig van Beethoven

Andante

Minuet

Luigi Boccherini

Moderato

TRIO

Sonata in A

Wolfgang Amadeus Mozart

Andante grazioso

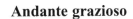

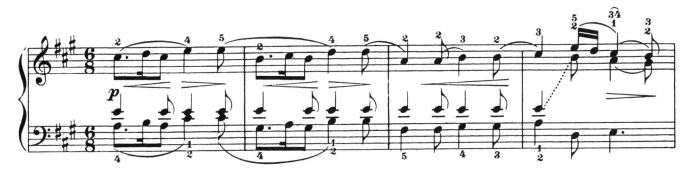

Piano Concerto No. 20

Wolfgang Amadeus Mozart

Andante

Piano Concerto No. 21

Wolfgang Amadeus Mozart

Andante

Rondo alla Turca

Wolfgang Amadeus Mozart

Allegretto

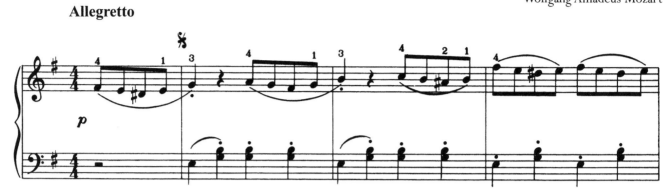

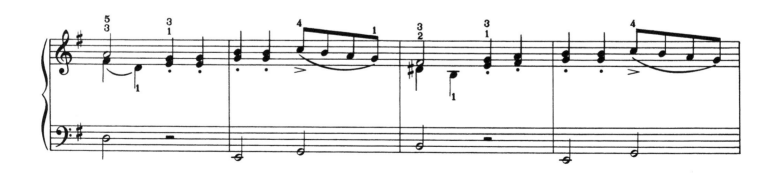

Sonata in C

Wolfgang Amadeus Mozart

Allegro

Tambourin

Jean-Philippe Rameau

Allegro moderato

Minuet

Jean-Philippe Rameau

Moderato

Waltz

Carl Maria von Weber

Moderato

D.C.

ROMANTIC FAVORITES

Hungarian Dance No. 5

Johannes Brahms

Allegro

Waltz

Johannes Brahms

Moderato

Fantaisie Impromptu

Frédéric Chopin

Moderato cantabile

Polonaise
Op. 40, No. 1

Frédéric Chopin

Moderato

Prelude

Op. 28, No. 4

Frédéric Chopin

Largo

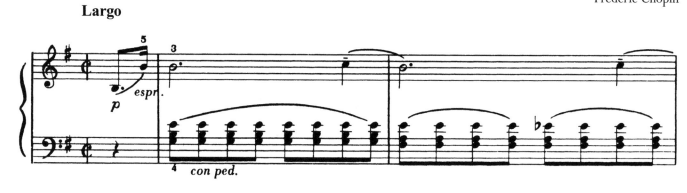

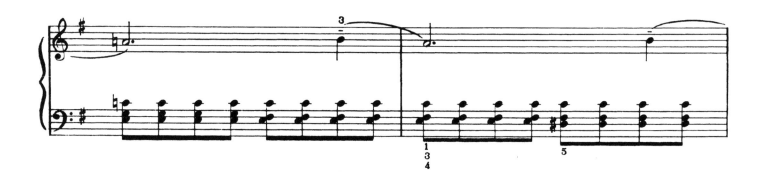

Waltz
Op. 64, No. 2

Frédéric Chopin

Moderato

Nocturne
Op. 9, No. 2

Frédéric Chopin

Andante

Clair de Lune

Claude Debussy

Rêverie

Claude Debussy

Andante

To a Wild Rose

Edward MacDowell

With simple tenderness

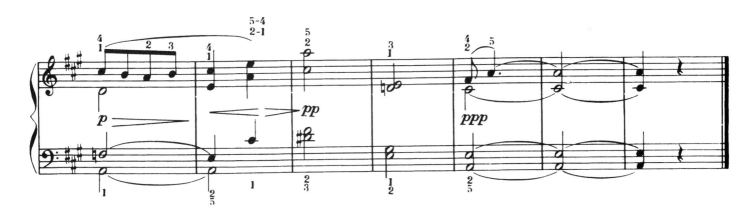

Liebesträum

Franz Liszt

Andantino dolce armonioso

Spring Song

Felix Mendelssohn

Allegretto grazioso

Melody in F

Anton Rubinstein

Marche Militaire

Franz Schubert

Allegro moderato

Serenade

Franz Schubert

Moderato

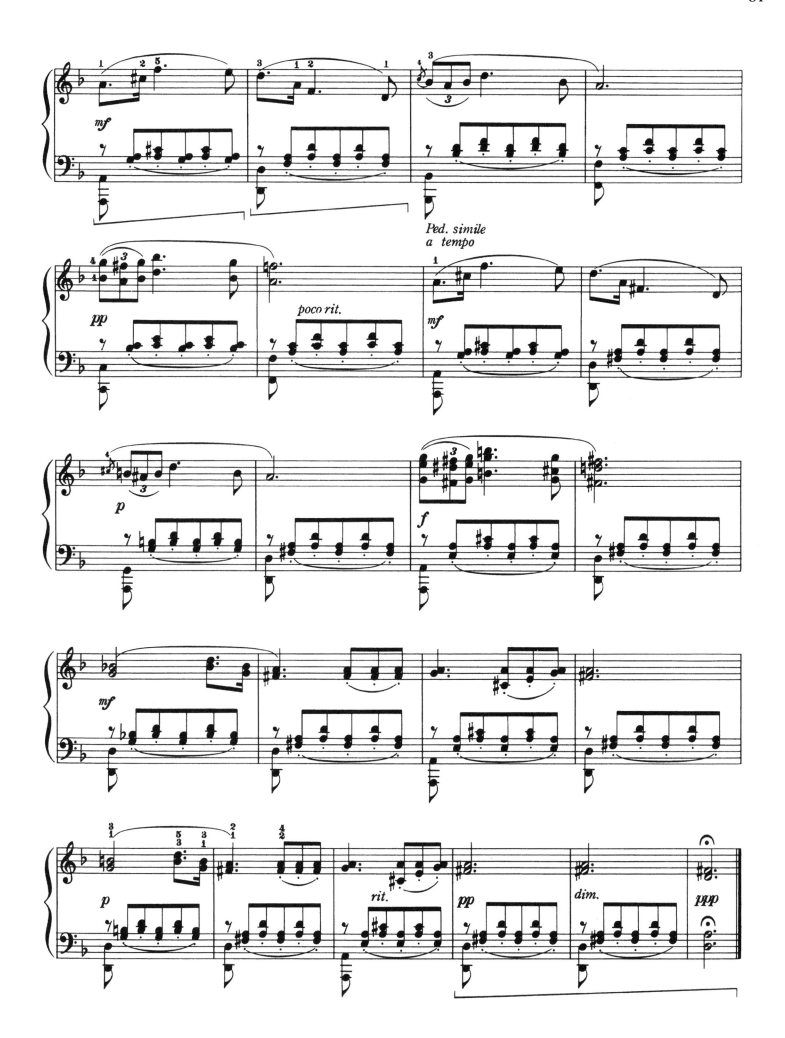

The Happy Farmer

Robert Schumann

Animato e grazioso

The Wild Horseman

Robert Schumann

Allegro con brio

Träumerei

Robert Schumann

Moderato espressivo

with Pedal

None But the Lonely Heart

Peter Ilyich Tchaikovsky

Andante con espressione

Piano Concerto No. 1

First Movement

Peter Ilyich Tchaikovsky

Allegro non troppo

Chanson Triste

Peter Ilyich Tchaikovsky

Andantino

CELEBRATE AMERICA

Over There

George M. Cohan

With a steady beat

Yankee Doodle Dandy

George M. Cohan

Moderato

You're a Grand Old Flag

George M. Cohan

Moderato

Tenting Tonight

William Kittridge

Moderately slow

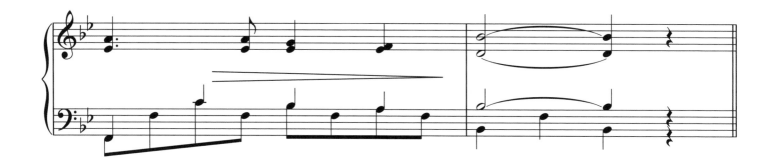

Thunder and Blazes

Julius Fučik

Marziale

TRIO

The Caissons Go Rolling Along

Edmund L. Gruber

Energetico

The American Patrol

F. W. Meacham

Energetico

She Wore a Yellow Ribbon

George A. Norton

With a steady beat

Keep the Home Fires Burning

Ivor Novello

Hail, Columbia

Philip Phile

Broadly

Hail to the Chief
(The President's March)

James Sanderson

With spirit

Rally Round the Flag

George F. Root

The Liberty Bell

John Philip Sousa

Allegro

D.S. al Fine

Semper Fidelis

John Philip Sousa

Energetico

Stars and Stripes Forever

John Philip Sousa

Moderato

D.C. al FINE
(without repeat)

The Washington Post

John Philip Sousa

Moderato con moto

The Star-Spangled Banner

John Stafford Smith

America
(My Country 'Tis of Thee)

Traditional

Andante

Battle Hymn of the Republic
(Glory Hallelujah)

Traditional

With a steady beat

The Marines' Hymn

from *The Halls of Montezuma*

Traditional

Marziale

The Red, White, and Blue
(Columbia, the Gem of the Ocean)

Traditional

Moderato

When Johnny Comes Marching Home

Traditional

Moderato

Yankee Doodle

Traditional

Brightly

Chorus

Anchors Aweigh

Charles A. Zimmerman

America, the Beautiful

Samuel A. Ward

ALL OVER THIS LAND

Carry Me Back to Old Virginny

James A. Bland

With feeling

Give My Regards to Broadway

George M. Cohan

Moderato

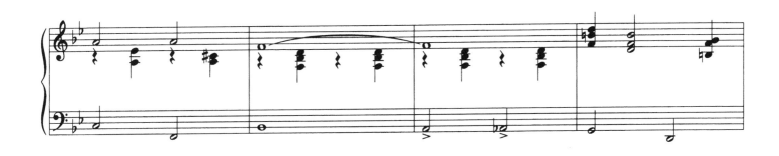

Way Down Yonder in New Orleans

Henry Creamer & J. Turner Layton

Moderato

Carolina in the Morning

Walter Donaldson

Moderato

On the Banks of the Wabash

Paul Dresser

Moderato

Chicago

Fred Fisher

Moderato

My Old Kentucky Home

Stephen Foster

Andantino

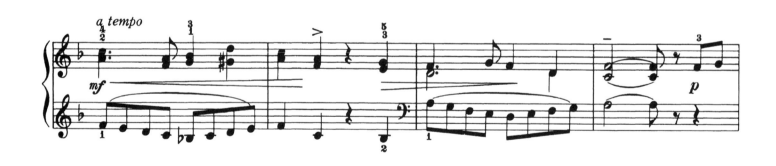

Way Down Upon the Swanee River

(Old Folks at Home)

Stephen Foster

Andantino

Kentucky Babe

Adam Geibel

Moderately slow

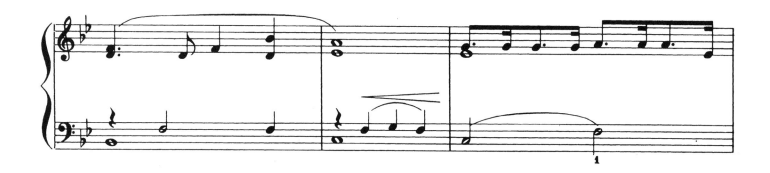

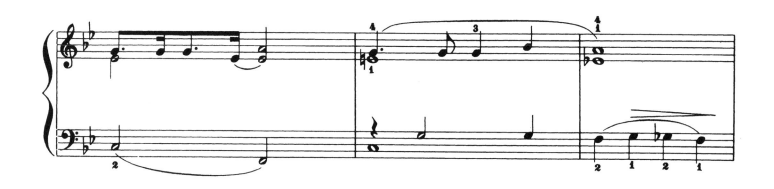

Swanee

George Gershwin

With energy

St. Louis Blues

W.C. Handy

Moderato

Chorus

Aloha Oe
(Farewell to Thee)

Queen Lydia Liliuokalani

With feeling

The Sidewalks of New York

Charles B. Lawlor & James W. Blake

With movement

Meet Me in St. Louis, Louis

Kerry Mills

Rock-a-Bye Your Baby with a Dixie Melody

Jean Schwartz

Moderato

a tempo

Home on the Range

Traditional

With movement

On Top of Old Smoky

H.S. Thompson

Gently

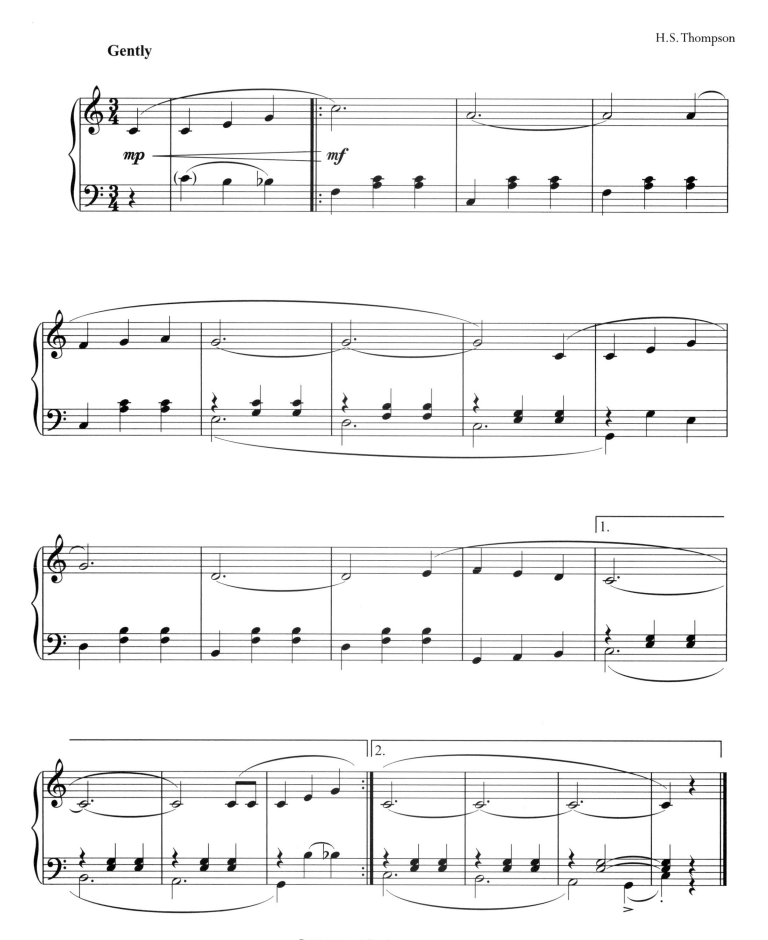

Red River Valley

Traditional

Moderato

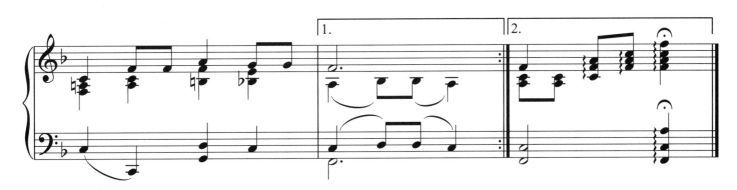

Shenandoah
(The Wide Missouri)

Traditional

Freely

The Yellow Rose of Texas

Traditional

With a steady beat

Dallas Blues

Spencer Williams

Slowly

Jazz Standards and Showstoppers

Alexander's Ragtime Band

Irving Berlin

With a steady beat

I Love a Piano

Irving Berlin

Moderato

A Pretty Girl Is Like a Melody

Irving Berlin

Moderato

Some of These Days

Shelton Brooks

Moderato

Bill Bailey

Hughie Cannon

Moderato

I'm Always Chasing Rainbows

Harry Carroll

After You've Gone

Henry Creamer & J. Turner Layton

I'll Build a Stairway to Paradise

George Gershwin

Energetico

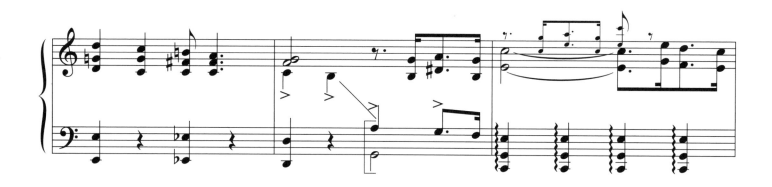

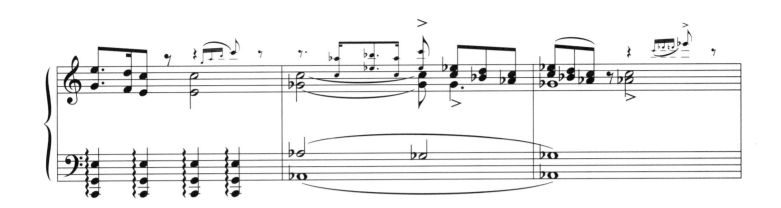

Pretty Baby

T. Jackson & Egbert van Alstyne

Moderato

I'm Forever Blowing Bubbles

Jaan Kenbrovin & J. W. Kellette

Moderately slow

They Didn't Believe Me

Jerome Kern

Gently

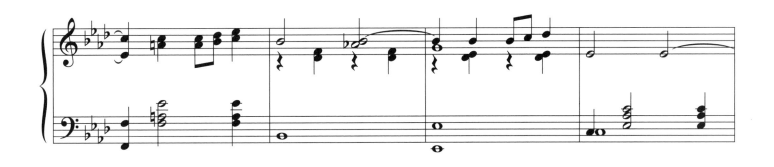

You Made Me Love You

James V. Monaco & Joseph McCarthy

Moderato

Ciribiribin

Alberto Pestalozza

With movement

Moonlight Bay

Percy Wenrich

With movement

Danny Boy

Traditional

Freely

Ain't We Got Fun

Richard Whiting

Moderato

In the Shade of the Old Apple Tree

Harry H. Williams & Egbert van Alstyne

Moderato

ORCHESTRAL THEMES

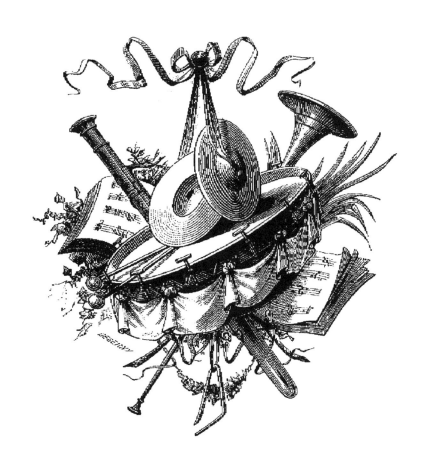

Air on the G String

Johann Sebastian Bach

Moderately slow

Jesu, Joy of Man's Desiring

Johann Sebastian Bach

Moderato

Symphony No. 7

Second Movement

Ludwig van Beethoven

Allegretto

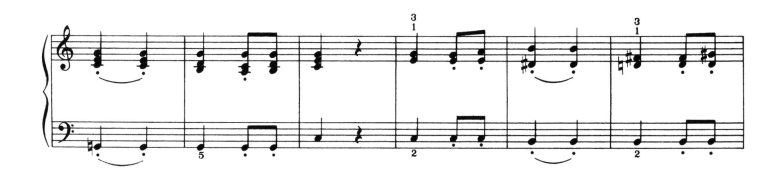

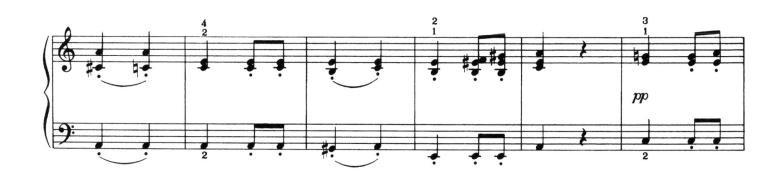

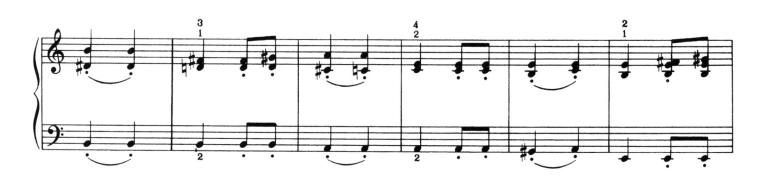

Eroica Symphony

Ludwig van Beethoven

Allegretto

Morning

from *Peer Gynt*

Edvard Grieg

Allegretto

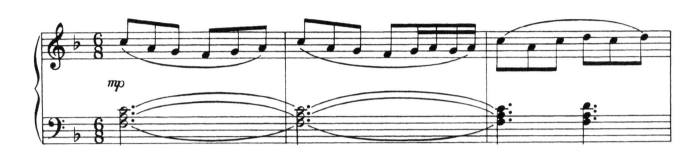

Symphony No. 9

Last Movement—Ode to Joy

Ludwig van Beethoven

Allegro moderato

New World Symphony

Antonín Dvořák

Majestically

Largo
from *Xerxes*

George Frideric Handel

Grandioso

Air

from *The Water Music*

George Frideric Handel

Con moto

Symphony No. 104

Second Movement—London

Franz Joseph Haydn

Moderato

Symphony No. 40
Theme

Wolfgang Amadeus Mozart

Moderato

Romance

from *Eine Kleine Nachtmusik*

Wolfgang Amadeus Mozart

Andante

Lacrimosa

from *Requiem*

Wolfgang Amadeus Mozart

Adagio

Barcarolle

from *Tales of Hoffman*

Jacques Offenbach

sempre più dolce   morendo

ppp

una corda

Canon

Johann Pachelbel

Smoothly

The Young Prince and the Young Princess

from *Sheherezade*

Nikolai Rimsky-Korsakov

Moderato

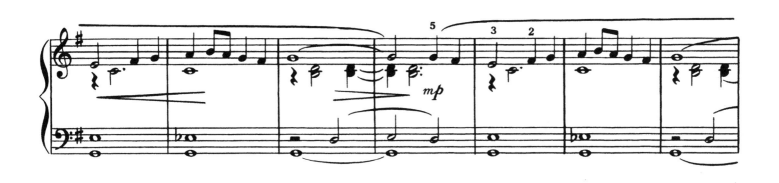

The Swan

Camille Saint-Saëns

Espressivo

Unfinished Symphony

Franz Schubert

Moderato

Waltz

from *Serenade for Strings*

Peter Ilyich Tchaikovsky

Moderato

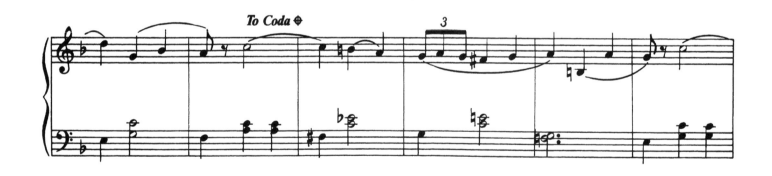

Symphony No. 5
Second Movement

Peter Ilyich Tchaikovsky

Andante cantabile

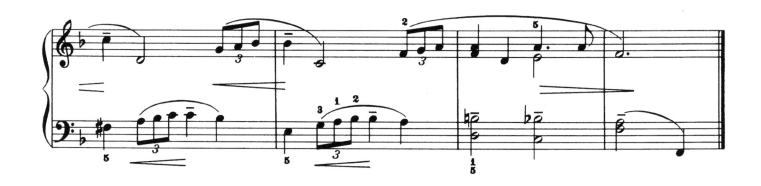

Symphony Pathétique

First Movement

Peter Ilyich Tchaikovsky

Andante

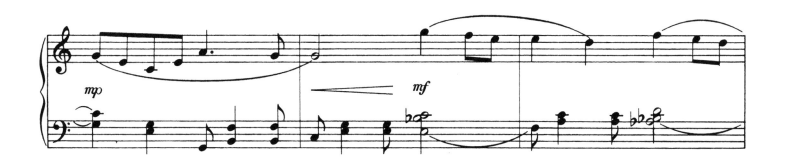

Andante Cantabile

from *Quartet in D*

Peter Ilyich Tchaikovsky

Freely

NOVELTY SOLOS

Habanera

from *Carmen*

Georges Bizet

Tango

Isaac Albéniz

Andantino

Bugle Call Rag

Eubie Blake

Moderato

Pizzicato

from *Sylvia*

Léo Delibes

Allegretto

The Chrysanthemum

Scott Joplin

252

The Entertainer

Scott Joplin

Moderato

254

Maple Leaf Rag

Scott Joplin

Not fast

Chopsticks

Arthur de Lulli

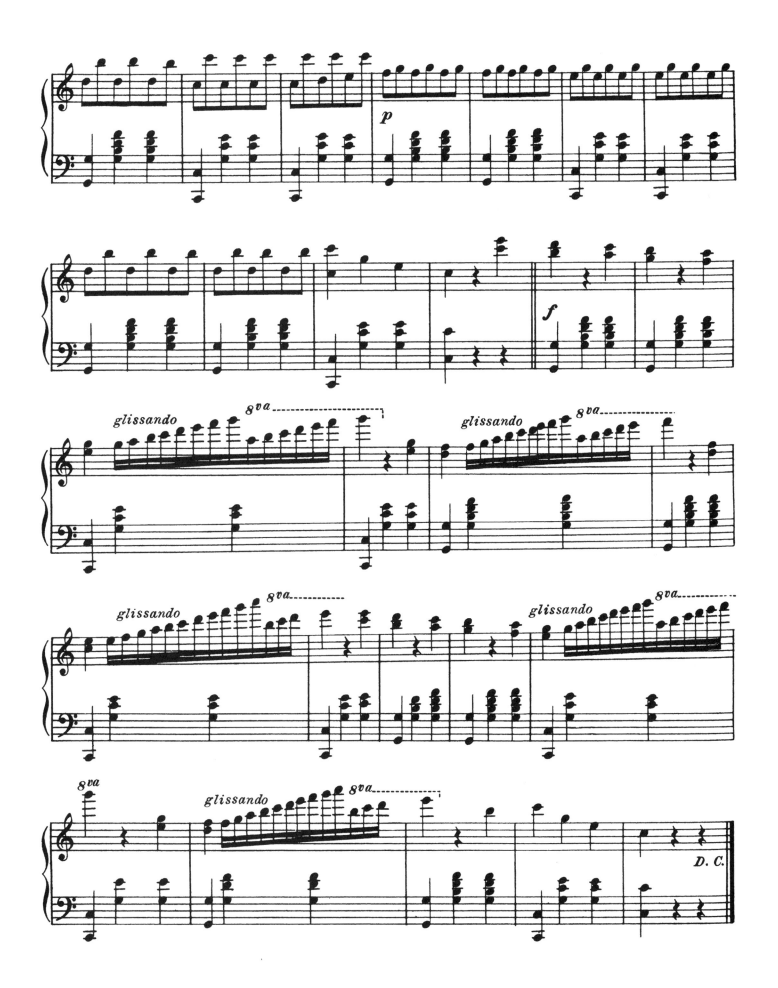

Glow Worm

Paul Lincke

Moderato

The Whistler and His Dog

Arthur Pryor

Moderate walking tempo

D.C. al Fine

Fascination

F.D. Marchetti

Con moto

Over the Waves

Juventino Rosas

Legato

Tales from the Vienna Woods

Johann Strauss

Legato

Fine

D.S. al Fine

Skaters Waltz

Emil Waldteufel

D.S. al fine

Blue Danube Waltz

Johann Strauss

Estudiantina

Emil Waldteufel

La Paloma
(The Dove)

Sebastian Yradier

Andante

HYMNS AND CELEBRATIONS

O Holy Night

Adolphe Adam

With feeling

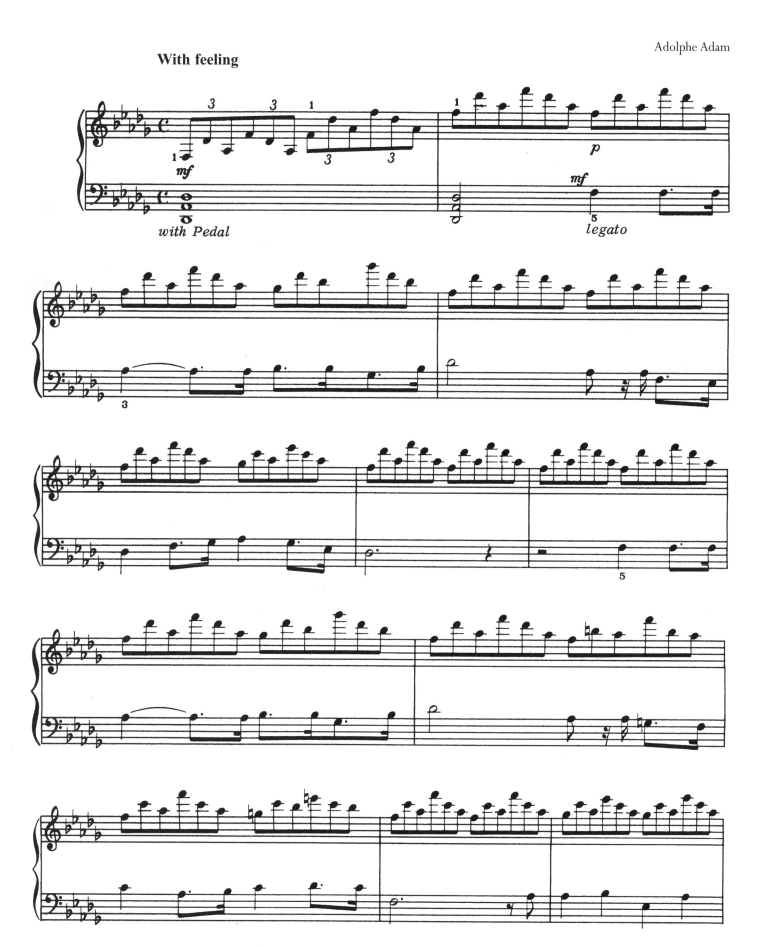

Sleepers Awake

Johann Sebastian Bach

Moderato tranquillo

Home, Sweet Home

Henry R. Bishop

Come, Ye Thankful People, Come

George J. Elvey

Moderato

The Golden Wedding

Gabriel-Marie

Allegro moderato

with Pedal

Silent Night

Franz Gruber

Sweetly

Hallelujah Chorus

from *Messiah*

George Frideric Handel

Allegro moderato

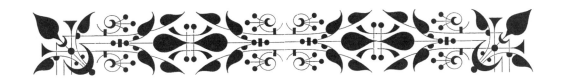

Anniversary Waltz
(Danube Waves)

Iosif Ivanovici

Moderato

Parade of the Tin Soldiers

Leon Jessell

Gracefully

D.C. al Fine

Wedding March

from *A Midsummer Night's Dream*

Felix Mendelssohn

Marcato maestoso

Brightest and Best
(Star of the East)

Felix Mendelssohn

Freely

Hark! the Herald Angels Sing

Felix Mendelssohn

Moderato

Dance of the Sugar Plum Fairy

from *The Nutcracker*

Peter Ilyich Tchaikovsky

Andante non troppo

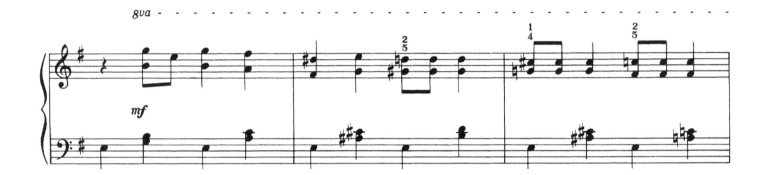

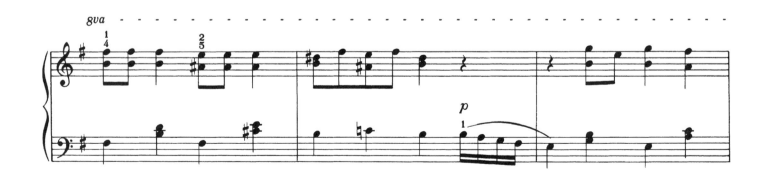

March

from *The Nutcracker*

Peter Ilyich Tchaikovsky

Moderato

Amazing Grace

Traditional

Freely

with Pedal

Havah Nagilah

Traditional

With vigor

Deep River

Traditional

Sweetly

What Child Is This?

Traditional

Sweetly

mp

with Pedal

Auld Lang Syne

Traditional

Moderato

When the Saints Go Marching In

Traditional

Moderato

O Come, All Ye Faithful

arr. Renaud de Vilbac

Andante

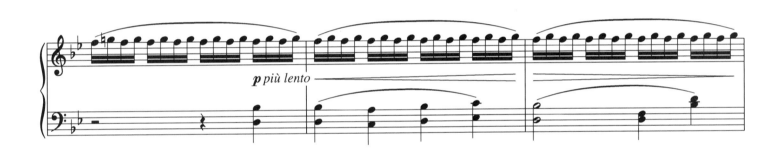

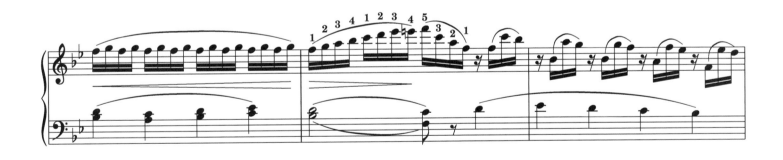

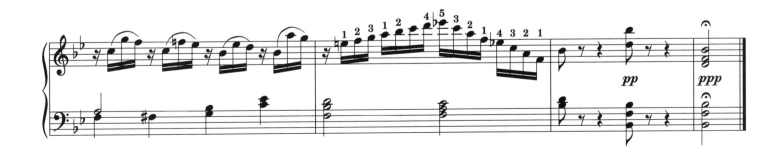

Bridal Chorus

from *Lohengrin*

Richard Wagner

Andante

INDEX